LOVE MESSAGES
FROM GOD

JENIL BENNETT

November Media Publishing
Chicago, IL.

November Media Publishing, Chicago IL.
Copyright © 2018 Jenil Bennett
All rights reserved. No part of this publication may be reproduced, distributed, or transmitted in any form or by any means, including photocopying, recording, or other electronic or mechanical methods, without the prior written permission of the publisher, except in the case of brief quotations embodied in critical reviews and certain other noncommercial uses permitted by copyright law. For permission requests, write to the publisher, addressed "Attention: Permissions Coordinator,"
at the email address below.

November Media
info@novembermediapublishing.com
Ordering Information: Special discounts are available on quantity purchases by corporations, associations, and others. For details, contact the publisher at the email address above.
Printed in the United States of America

Produced & Published By November Media Publishing
ISBN: 978-0-9998274-4-4

Scripture references: ERV, NIV, NLT, MSG, AMP, ESV, ISV
First Edition : April 2018
10 9 8 7 6 5 4 3 2 1

A note from the Author:

The purpose of this book is to remind all people of the Love God has for them and the truth of His Love. This book is also a tool to facilitate reading God's word. However, this is not your typical book. Each page contains a love message from God. You can randomly choose a page to read. Each page can be torn out, so it can be given to someone or be kept with you throughout the day. On the back of each message there is a journal page. This is so you can write any thoughts or prayers.

It is my prayer that God's Holy Spirit permeates every page and blesses the life of every person that touches this book. In Jesus' Name. Amen

Enjoy and God bless you,

-Jenil

I've planned good things for you to do. I've planned good things for you to go through. I've planned for some good things to happen to you. So, don't be afraid. Face life head on, not timid or dreadful. Don't be so in your emotions. Just trust me. Enjoy me. I love you.

Ephesians 2:10 ERV

*Let HIS light shine through you,
by simply being you.*

JOHN 1:4 ERV

I lead, and I protect.
I guide, and I deliver.
And it's all because I love you.

So, don't be afraid and don't give up hoping in me. I'm the only thing that's secure. I'm the only one that's secure. I'm secure in who I am. And I'm secure in what I will do. I'm a secure foundation for you. I'm a secure foundation for your hopes. I'm a secure foundation for love.

So, you want to love better. You want to experience my love better. You want your family to know my love. Then just come to me. Much love is in me. Trust that I know just what to do. Trust that I know just how to do it. What are you looking forward to? That's the very thing that you trust in me for. I know just what to do. And I know just how to do it.

I lead, and I protect.
I guide, and I deliver.
And it's all because I love you.

(<u>Your name</u>). I love you. Remember that I love you. In all things, remember that I love you!

ISAIAH 43 NIV

I am you. Just listen to that. I…am… you. I AM equals you.

You are not me. I am the great I AM. I am fluid and can be whatever I choose to be. I am whatever you need me to be. Everything is what it is because of me. I am in everything. Therefore, I am in you. I am you. The great I AM is in you. You are nothing without me. You are because of me. You've been needing strength. I AM is in you, which gives you strength. Anything else you need, you can have, because I AM is in you. There are no limits to who I can be for you. There are no limits to who I can be through you. I would not ask you to give of yourself if I didn't know what is in you. Anything I need you to be, you will be through me. So, believe that I am you.

JOHN 1:3 ERV

EXODUS 3:14 NLT

If you have a dream, give it to God then go for it! If it's in His will for you, he'll direct and instruct you. If it's not, he'll tell you so. Trust Him- through the risk, the obstacles, and uncertainties. Don't quit just because it gets hard.

PROVERBS 16:3 ISV

1 SAMUEL 18:14 NIV

GENESIS 39:2 NLT

PSALMS 32:8 NIV

U R A CHILD OF GOD…

enough said!

JOHN 1:12 ESV

ROMANS 8:28-31 ERV

Don't worry. JESUS is NEVER blind to your tears, NEVER deaf to your prayers, and NEVER silent to your pain. He sees, He hears, He answers… And He WILL deliver you!!!

Trust Him…

2 THESSALONIANS 3:3 NLT

PSALMS 145:18-19 ERV

Pay attention to how you talk to yourself.

Pay attention to what you think about yourself.

Pay attention to how you view yourself.

Pay attention to what you tell yourself.

It has everything to do with your health.

It has everything to do with your peace.

ROMANS 8:6 NIV

I give you permission to do nothing. You can do nothing, and all hell can break loose, and you will be safe! The very things you have been wondering how to do are the very things you need not do. I have you secured.

REVELATIONS 12:14-17 NIV

(Your Name). I appreciate you. There's nothing you've done. But, I just appreciate you. Everything about you, I appreciate. You may make mistakes; don't always make the mark. You may even feel like there's so much more you can do. But, I just want you to know I appreciate you! I appreciate you being open and willing to be you. In this day and time when people aren't willing to be their authentic selves- it's great to see you be the wonderful you. You're free in just being you. And that I appreciate!

PSALMS 147:11 NLT

ZEPHANIAH 3:17 NLT

(Your Name). You don't have to know every step to take. You don't have to know the outcome. You just have to know that in-between there is you- perfectly in my arms.

ISAIAH 41:13 NIV

PSALMS 32:8 NIV

Let God love you through this.

EPHESIANS 3:18 NLT

(Your name). It's not about feelings. Stop believing things based on your feelings. Focus on the facts. It's a fact that I'm always here with you. So, how can you say you feel so separate from me? It's a fact that we are one. I am in you, and you are in me. It's a fact that I love you. Even if you knew nothing about me and didn't even know to acknowledge me, it doesn't change the fact that I LOVE YOU! So, stop letting your feelings dictate your truth. Focus on my facts.

DEUTERONOMY 31:6 ESV

1 CORINTHIANS 6:17 NIV

JOHN 3:16

EPHESIANS 1:3-6 MSG

You are precious. One of great value,
not to be wasted or treated carelessly.

Love,

~ God

ISAIAH 43:4 ESV

MALACHI 3:17 NLT

Don't let <u>anyone</u> dim your light.

JOHN 1:4-5 NIV

I want you to focus on all my great promises. There are so many great promises for you in the Bible! Satan will distract you with problems. But it's ok. He's doing what he is supposed to do. Now you get to focus on my promises, rather than the problems. It's like he set you up for a good outcome. The moment Satan presents a problem; you get to run in the opposite direction towards a promise! And the great thing about it is that any promise will do! It doesn't matter which promise you run to, because you are safe with all my promises.

My promises will be your protection from your worst fears. My promises will be your peace and strength. My promises will be the answers to the questions in your soul. My promises will be your access to me. No. You don't have to think about the problems. You don't have to figure it out. I've already promised you I will perfect everything that concerns you. I've already promised you I have a great future ahead of you. I've already promised you I am always here for you, and absolutely nothing can stop my LOVE for you!

Satan is just a bully, and he likes to poke you with problems. I am just love, and I like to wrap you in my promises.

2 PETER 1:4 NLT
1 PETER 5:8 NIV

(Your name). You are brilliant. You are excellent. You have such a great swag and aura of positivity! That's who you are, and that's what I want you to focus on today and every day. Continue to think on all the great things about you! Don't let the negativity of life draw you in. Don't become timid or dim your light. These obstacles are here for you to overcome and shine brighter in the face of adversity. Yes, you are meant to shine brighter in the face of adversity! When you're opposed, let your light shine. When you're speaking, let your light shine. When you're afraid, let your light shine. In all things you do, be the radiant you that you are! And I will be pleased.

MATTHEW 5:14-16 NLT

IN ALL THINGS GIVE THANKS!!!

1 THESSALONIANS 5:16-18 NLT

Don't be afraid to step out. You have an idea; go for it! It's not a matter of wrong or right or what I want you to do or don't want you to do. You were once at the stage of a young toddler playing at the park. You needed me to hold your hand and guide you through every part of the park. But now, you've matured and no longer need that. I'm like the Parent that can sit on the park bench and enjoy watching you play. And that's what I want you to do. Play! Enjoy each moment, whether you know what it will be or not. Although I'm not holding your hand and telling you what to do each step, know that I am still right here.

I'm never leaving, and my loving eye is on you. Eventually, you'll be the child that runs ahead of their Parent into the park. But still, I will never leave you. I will never let you run too far ahead. If you happen to run off into trouble or danger, I'm still coming to get you and take you back to safety. Then one day, you'll walk yourself to the park, and still, you won't be without me. I'll be the Parent that's waiting for you patiently at home. You'll always be able to come to me, and I'll always be able to find you. So, don't be afraid to enjoy life.

PSALMS 139:3-10 NLT

Do something for you…. TODAY!

MARK 12:30-31 ERV

There's an expectation in accepting God's love; and that is to love others.

1 JOHN 4:11-12 NLT

All I want you to do is accept my love. When your heart feels shaky and your mind worries, that's an opportunity to accept my love. Don't be afraid; just step out and accept my love. At the end of it all is my love. Once you're done with all your worries, and your frustrations have subsided- there will be my love. So why don't you bypass all of that and step into my love. Come on and step into my love. Come on and step out on my love. Come on, take a plunge and try my love. No need to be afraid. No need to be afraid.

The foundation of everything is my love. At the foundation of all your hopes, all your fears, all your desires, all your decisions- is my love. Don't be afraid to step out onto my love. My love is secure; come on in my love. Oh, come on and rest in my love. Oh, I love you (your name). I love you with an untainted endless love. So, come on and step out on my love.

PROVERBS 3:5-6 ERV
JEREMIAH 32:27 ERV
EXODUS 14:13 ERV

44

*(Your name). You are so beautiful.
There is so much beauty in you.*

SONG OF SOLOMON 4:7 ERV

U R GOOD ENOUGH...
and that's enough!

HEBREWS 13:21 NLT

COLOSSIANS 2:10 ERV

ALL IS WELL.

2 KINGS 4:26 ESV

50

Just hit it with the word!

When negative thoughts keep wanting to pop in your mind or your mind wants to wander off and take control... Just hit it with the word. Pretend your thoughts are like those little frogs in the game at the arcade. Every time they pop up, the goal is to hit them with a ball until they are knocked down. That's all you have to do. The enemy is just presenting an opportunity for you to knock him down!

2 CORINTHIANS.10.3-5.NLT

ROMANS.8.6.NIV

IN ALL THINGS PRAISE HIM!!!

1 THESSALONIANS 5:18 NIV

PSALMS 34:1-3 NLT

I am requiring you to become good at "being in me". Become proficient at just being. You're good at: doing, and keeping things going, and always having something to do. But it's the "being" that counts. Look up what it means to "be".

Be means to exist or live in.

Being means God- Absolute existence in a complete or perfect state, lacking no essential characteristic, essence.

You can do everything through me. Not in your own way and power but through me and my ways, the pace I would do it in. The way I think about it. Do everything with my Spirit. When I say "just be", it doesn't mean you aren't doing anything. To "just be" is to be relaxed, in the moment, enjoying what you're doing in the moment and not rushed.

PROVERBS 4:10 NLT

JESUS LOVES YOU…

enough said.

ROMANS 8:35-39 NLT

(Your name). I love you. That's all I want you to focus on. My love is everlasting, and my love endures always. But, what are you doing with my love? Are you focusing on it? Look for the ways I love you. Look for my presence. Look for how I am at work in your situations. It's all right here- just look. Look expectantly for my love.

PSALMS 100:5 ERV

JEREMIAH 29:11-13 ERV

NO FEAR. Accept my perfect LOVE.

1 JOHN 4:16-18 NLT

EPHESIANS 3:18 NLT

There's beauty in every season. Not everyone enjoys the fall leaves, the cold of winter, the rain of spring, or the heat of summer. But, for some, each season is enjoyable, based on perspective. You can see the beauty of the burgundy and orange leaves if you focus on that. There can be pleasure in the discomfort of the rain if you allow for that. You can find joy in whatever season, based on what you choose to focus on. Going through seasons are just a process of life. No matter how much it rains or pours, you're kept safe. And when the unexpected change happens in the season, it will never change the fact that the Sun is always there. Even when the sky all around is blue and grey, the sun is still there behind the thick of the clouds. In your seasons of life, focus your hope on my Son; He is always there. Look for the beauty in every season. When you focus your hope on my Son, and you look for the beauty in every season, you can make it through life pleasantly.

ECCLESIASTES 3:11 NLT

No matter how smooth or rough this day is, God is ALWAYS with me.

PSALMS 139:10 NLT

There is **NOTHING**, absolutely **NOTHING**, too hard for **GOD!**

JEREMIAH 32:27 NIV

Look forward to the Holy Spirit's work in your life, in your family's life. I want your family to live for me just as much as you do. You feel the way you do because I am in you. So, don't focus on what you see and feel right now. Don't focus on what has not yet been developed. Focus on the promise of the Holy Spirit. I will see to it that their lives are given to me. The Holy Spirit will see to it that they continue to live for me.

JOHN 14:15-17,23 NIV,
JEREMIAH 31:33-37 ERV

The TRUTH is… YOU came into life as a WINNER!!!

ROMANS 8:37 NLT

Live your life with me at the forefront of your mind. No worries. No fears. No timidity. Don't let anything become stronger in your life. Don't let anything occupy your mind and heart more than me. This is how you worship me. Just know that I love you.

2 TIMOTHY 1:7 AMP

Do something for you…. TODAY!

MATTHEW 22:39 ERV

Sit and be still.

PSALMS 127 : 2 NLT

In each moment, I'm dating you. Let's just enjoy life together.

EZEKIEL 16:8 NIV

Choose to be content.

PHILIPPIANS 4:11-13 ERV

I am guiding you along the best pathway for your life. I am advising you and watching over you.

PSALMS 32:8 NLT

You can make a mistake. Free yourself to make a mistake. Give yourself grace when you make a mistake. I did everything right, so you wouldn't have to! That's too much pressure to be right all the time. You're going to do wrong, and it's ok. You're going to slip up, and it's ok. You're going to miss the mark at times, and it's ok. That's why I gave my life. For those moments. So, you could still walk with your heart and your head held high. So, shame and accusations could not reign over you. I gave my life, so you could live free! Free of charges. Free of fear. Free of un-forgiveness. Free to make a mistake.

ROMANS 5:6 ERV

FORGIVE

COLOSSIANS 3:12-14 NLT

Forgiveness is choosing to give, despite their faults. For their rudeness, you give kindness. For their mistake, you give mercy. For their hatred, you give love.

JAMES 2:12-13 ERV

Don't let your soul be down or heavy.
Just put your hope and trust in God.

PSALMS 42:11 ERV

YOU'RE NATURALLY FLY!

PSALMS 139:14-16 MSG

Follow God's leading. You're on his escalator, no need for you to put in effort. He's in control. At the right time, He'll get you to the right level, where He'll need you to get off and put in effort. (Walk around and do what is needed to be done). Meanwhile, stop, be still, and focus on enjoying the escalator.

PROVERBS 1:33 NIV

I'm still here. You'll always be mine. I adore you. Why are you afraid? Don't be.

PSALMS 139:5 ERV

PSALMS 144:2 ERV

I LOVE YOU

EPHESIANS 1:4 NLT

JOHN 3:16 ERV

1 JOHN 4:9-10 NIV

100